I0815093

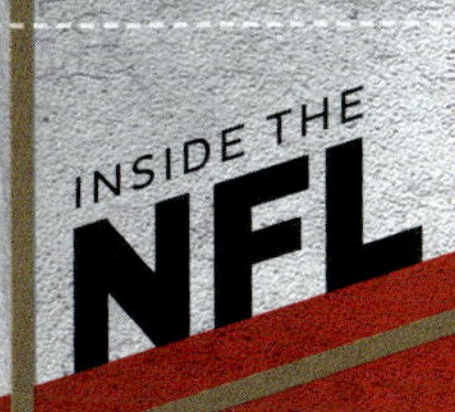

SAN FRANCISCO 49ERS

BY TONY HUNTER

SportsZone

An Imprint of Abdo Publishing
abdobooks.com

abdobooks.com

Published by Abdo Publishing, a division of ABDO, PO Box 398166, Minneapolis, Minnesota 55439.

Printed in the United States of America, North Mankato, Minnesota
022019
092019

Cover Photo: Tony Avelar/AP Images
Interior Photos: NFL Photos/AP Images, 5, 20; Lennox McLendon/AP Images, 7; AP Images, 11, 19, 23; Harry Harris/AP Images, 13, 43; Pro Football Hall of Fame/NFL Photos/AP Images, 15; Peter Read Miller/AP Images, 25; Susan Ragan/AP Images, 29; Bob Galbraith/AP Images, 31; Kevin Terrell/AP Images, 34–35; Jeff Chiu/AP Images, 37; Paul Abell/AP Images, 39; Charlie Riedel/AP Images, 41

Editor: Patrick Donnelly
Series Designer: Craig Hinton

Library of Congress Control Number: 2018965959

Publisher's Cataloging-in-Publication Data

Names: Hunter, Tony, author.
Title: San Francisco 49ers / by Tony Hunter
Description: Minneapolis, Minnesota: Abdo Publishing, 2020 | Series: Inside the NFL | Includes online resources and index.
Identifiers: ISBN 9781532118630 (lib. bdg.) | ISBN 9781532172816 (ebook)
Subjects: LCSH: San Francisco 49ers (Football team)--Juvenile literature. | National Football League--Juvenile literature. | Football teams--Juvenile literature. | American football--Juvenile literature.
Classification: DDC 796.33264--dc23

TABLE OF CONTENTS

CHAPTER 1

CONTINUED GREATNESS

The 75,129 fans at Joe Robbie Stadium in Miami, Florida, could sense what was about to happen. With 3:20 left, the Cincinnati Bengals led the San Francisco 49ers 16–13 in Super Bowl XXIII. The 49ers had the ball, but they were on their own 8-yard line. They needed a field goal to tie or a touchdown to win. The Bengals just had to stop them. But that was easier said than done.

San Francisco had relied heavily on its dynamic offense during the 1988 season. Quarterback Joe Montana was considered one of the best in the National Football League (NFL). Running back Roger Craig had a career-high 2,036 total yards of offense that season. Future Hall of Fame wide receiver Jerry Rice was just coming into his prime.

49ers quarterback Joe Montana drops back to search for an open receiver during Super Bowl XXIII.

But throughout the game, the Bengals defense held the 49ers mostly in check.

The Niners defense also held strong, however, and at halftime the game was tied 3–3. Each team added a field goal in the third quarter to stay even at 6–6. But then Cincinnati's Stanford Jennings returned a kickoff 93 yards for a touchdown to close out the third quarter.

That woke up the 49ers offense. Montana drove the team 85 yards in four plays. He finished the drive with a 14-yard touchdown pass to Rice. But Cincinnati answered when Jim Breech made his third field goal of the day with 3:20 to play.

With the Bengals ahead 16–13, Montana led the 49ers offense back onto the field. They were 92 yards away from the Bengals' end zone. Without the slightest sign of nerves, Montana began the drive. One play after another, he moved the offense down the field. Montana connected

WELCOME TO THE HALL OF FAME

Many credit coach Bill Walsh for San Francisco's dominance during the 1980s. But he certainly had a lot of talented players to work with, too. The roster included six future Hall of Fame players. They were Joe Montana, Jerry Rice, Steve Young, Ronnie Lott, Charles Haley, and Fred Dean. Walsh is also in the Hall of Fame.

Jerry Rice makes a fingertip catch during Super Bowl XXIII.

with Rice three times. The last of these was a 27-yard strike to put the 49ers in the red zone.

The Bengals figured Montana would try to go to Rice again, this time in the end zone. But the quarterback had other plans. Montana hit wide receiver John Taylor for a 10-yard touchdown pass with 34 seconds left on the clock. Taylor's touchdown capped off an 11-play, 92-yard drive, and San Francisco held on to win 20–16.

It is hard to believe that the 49ers were ever losing the game. San Francisco had 452 offensive yards that day to Cincinnati's 229. Rice, named the game's Most Valuable Player (MVP), set a Super Bowl record with 215 receiving yards while catching 11 passes. Montana also set a Super Bowl record with 357 passing yards.

The 49ers were a dominant team during the 1980s. The thrilling drive in January 1989 secured the team's third Super Bowl victory. The first two had also come during that decade. The fourth came just 12 months later in a 55–10 romp over the Denver Broncos.

The 49ers showcased their celebrated passing attack in their Super Bowl wins. Head coach Bill Walsh was its mastermind.

ROGER CRAIG

Roger Craig was the 49ers' top running back during their era of greatness in the 1980s. He was known for his high-knee running style. During the 1985 season, he became the first NFL player to rush for 1,000 yards while also tallying 1,000 receiving yards during the same season. Craig also became the first player to score three touchdowns in a Super Bowl, which he did in Super Bowl XIX against the Miami Dolphins. He was named the NFL Offensive Player of the Year in 1988.

JOE COOL AND JERRY RICE

Joe Montana had a reputation for being cool under pressure. Jerry Rice is widely regarded as the greatest receiver to ever play the game. Together they helped the 49ers offense shred opposing defenses for years.

Over the course of his 15-year career, Montana led his teams to 31 fourth-quarter comebacks. The former University of Notre Dame star also threw for more than 40,000 yards and 273 touchdowns. Montana was named MVP of three Super Bowls and was selected to eight Pro Bowls.

Rice came out of Mississippi Valley State, a school that played one level below the major college programs. He made an immediate impact as a pro, earning National Football Conference (NFC) Offensive Rookie of the Year honors in 1985. Rice became only the third receiver to earn MVP honors in the Super Bowl. Montana entered the Pro Football Hall of Fame in 2000. Rice was inducted in 2010.

Defenses feared the 49ers throughout the 1980s. If Montana was not passing to one of his star receivers—Rice, Taylor, or Dwight Clark—he was handing the ball or passing it to Craig, one of the most versatile running backs in NFL history.

Although the team was known for its offense, the 49ers had a strong defense, too. Anchored by defensive backs Ronnie Lott and Eric Wright, the defense made sure its presence was also felt. The glory years of the 1980s showed just how high the 49ers had risen since the team's humble beginning in the late 1940s.

CHAPTER 2

THE GOLD RUSH

Anthony J. "Tony" Morabito had a vision. He wanted to bring football to northern California. The San Francisco businessman believed that a pro football team could thrive on the West Coast. At the time, there were no major pro sports teams west of the Mississippi River.

Morabito tried unsuccessfully to acquire an NFL franchise between 1941 and 1946. After those failed attempts, Morabito decided to pursue a team in the rival All-America Football Conference (AAFC). The 49ers became charter members of the AAFC. The team was named in honor of the miners who rushed west in search of gold in 1849.

The 49ers made their regular-season debut at home on September 8, 1946, losing to the New York Yankees 21–7 at Kezar Stadium. San Francisco finished 9–5 that year and

R. C. Owens demonstrates his famous alley-oop catch during a 1957 practice.

8–4–2 during the next season, good for second place each season.

Niners fans had high hopes as the 1948 campaign played out. San Francisco won its first 10 games, setting up a showdown with the Cleveland Browns. The Browns were the defending AAFC champions and also came into the game undefeated. Playing at home, the Browns forced six 49ers turnovers and pulled out a 14–7 victory.

ALL-AMERICA FOOTBALL CONFERENCE

The AAFC began with eight teams in 1946. The New York Yankees, Brooklyn Dodgers, Buffalo Bisons, and Miami Seahawks made up the Eastern Division. The Cleveland Browns, Chicago Rockets, Los Angeles Dons, and San Francisco 49ers played in the Western Division. The Browns won the league title in each of the four years of the AAFC's existence.

The rivals met again two weeks later back in San Francisco. The 49ers needed to beat the Browns to stay in contention for the league championship. San Francisco held a 21–10 lead in the third quarter, but three touchdown passes by Cleveland's Otto Graham put the Browns on top 31–21. The Niners fought back with a touchdown pass from Frankie Albert to Joe Perry, but it was not enough. Cleveland remained undefeated and won the division title with its 31–28 victory. The Browns were the only team to beat the Niners during their 12–2 season.

Running back John Strzykalski scores a touchdown at New York in 1951.

The 49ers got a chance for revenge during the next season. The league did away with divisions in 1949 and added a second round of playoffs. The four best teams qualified. The Niners split two games with the Browns in the regular season and finished in second place. After defeating the third-place New York Yankees at Kezar Stadium, the 49ers were to face Cleveland in the championship game. A few days before the game, the NFL and AAFC announced a merger. Three AAFC teams—the 49ers, the Browns, and the Baltimore Colts—would join the NFL. That meant the 49ers-Browns championship game would be the last game in the AAFC.

THE ESHMONT AWARD

The Eshmont Award is the highest honor a San Francisco 49ers player can earn. The award is given to the player who best displays the type of courageous and inspirational play shown by Len Eshmont, who played for the 49ers from 1946 to 1949. Eshmont was a running back and defensive back with the team. A former standout at Fordham University, Eshmont rushed for close to 1,200 yards and made 10 interceptions during his career with the 49ers.

After falling behind 14–0, the 49ers tried to rally. In the fourth quarter, they drove 74 yards down the field. Albert capped off the drive with a 23-yard touchdown pass to receiver Paul Salata. But that was all the 49ers could manage. The Browns ended up winning 21–7.

Coming into their NFL debut, the 49ers still had many of the star players who had almost won the 1949 AAFC title. But the New York Yanks spoiled the 49ers' first game with a 21–17 win. Although the 49ers racked up more passing and rushing yards that day, they were doomed by four turnovers. The 49ers were slow to recover from that first setback. They ended their first season in the NFL with a 3–9 record.

San Francisco brought in quarterback Y. A. Tittle in 1951. The team had four winning seasons as Tittle gradually replaced Albert as the starting quarterback. Perry had back-to-back 1,000-yard rushing seasons in 1953 and 1954 as the 49ers offense really started to click.

Hall of Famers Joe Perry (34) and Leo Nomellini (73) take the field before a game at Kezar Stadium.

The 49ers had their best season of their first decade in the NFL in 1957. They opened the season with a 20–10 loss to the Chicago Cardinals, but they won their next three games. That led to a showdown with the Chicago Bears on October 27.

Y. A. AND R. C.

Y. A. Tittle and R. C. Owens provided plenty of highlights for 49ers fans in the 1950s. Tittle was the 1948 rookie of the year with the Baltimore Colts in the AAFC. He joined the 49ers in 1951, after the Colts disbanded. During his 10 seasons in San Francisco, he threw for more than 16,000 yards and 108 touchdowns. He joined the New York Giants in 1961 and finished his career there. Tittle won NFL MVP honors in 1957, 1961, 1962, and 1963 and also played in seven Pro Bowls.

Owens joined the 49ers in 1957 and stayed there for the next five seasons. He is remembered in San Francisco as one of the most exciting players in team history. During his time there, he racked up 2,926 yards and 20 touchdown catches. Tittle and Owens were most famous for their alley-oop pass in which Owens would jump over defenders to catch the ball. The play became a staple of the 49ers offense during that era.

San Francisco fell behind 17–7. At that point, Morabito suffered a fatal heart attack in the stands. The heartbroken 49ers rallied to win, dedicating the 21–17 victory to their fallen owner.

The 49ers played another thriller against the Detroit Lions a week later. Tittle threw a 41-yard pass in the fourth quarter. R. C. Owens leaped up over two defenders to make the catch in the end zone. The 49ers escaped with a 35–31 victory. The play was known as the alley-oop pass and was used often by Tittle and Owens.

The Niners and the Lions finished the season tied atop the West Division standings with identical 8–4 records. That set up a one-game playoff to see who would face the East champion Browns for the NFL title. Behind Tittle's three touchdown passes, the 49ers surged to a 27–7 lead in the third quarter. But the Lions roared back and crushed the 49ers' championship dream. They ended up winning 31–27. That began a stretch of mediocrity for the 49ers that lingered for more than a decade.

The 49ers wouldn't win more than seven games in a season again until 1970. Albert had come back as head coach in 1956. After three seasons, he resigned and was replaced by Red Hickey, who guided the 49ers to back-to-back 7–5 records at the end of the 1950s. However, his most important contribution to football had little to do with wins and losses.

In 1960, the 49ers started the season 4–4. A game against the mighty Colts was on the horizon. The 49ers had a surprise in store for the Colts. Up until that point, quarterbacks usually received the snap while standing just behind the center. Against Baltimore, Hickey decided to have his quarterback stand five yards behind the center at the start of the play. The offensive formation gave the 49ers an extra second or two to develop a play. Hickey also believed it would give the 49ers a chance to knock off the Colts in Baltimore.

The formation was called the shotgun, and the plan worked. The 49ers exploded for more than 200 passing yards behind the play of quarterback John Brodie. But legendary Colts quarterback Johnny Unitas also had a stellar game. He passed for 356 yards. Brodie had to be taken out of the game with an injury. But with the Niners trailing 22–20, rookie quarterback Bob Waters hit Owens for a 21-yard touchdown to take the lead. The 49ers held on to earn a stunning 30–22 victory.

Defenses, however, soon adjusted to the shotgun offense. Hickey abandoned it in favor of the old T-formation. The shotgun was not used again until 1975, when the Dallas Cowboys tried it. Today it is a popular formation in both professional and college football.

Brodie's best year came in 1965. He set career highs with 3,112 passing yards and 30 touchdown passes. The 49ers had the top offense in the league that season, but they still finished with a 7–6–1 record.

Dick Nolan took over as head coach in 1968, and two years later the 49ers' fortunes changed. They went 10–3–1 and won their first NFC West Division title in 1970. They also won their first playoff game, a 17–14 victory on the road against the Minnesota Vikings. They came up one game short of the

San Francisco quarterback John Brodie looks for a receiver in a 1963 game against the Minnesota Vikings.

Super Bowl, losing to the Dallas Cowboys 17–10 in the NFC Championship Game. Brodie was named the NFL MVP in 1970. He threw for more than 2,900 yards and 24 touchdowns. 49ers cornerback Bruce Taylor was named the league's defensive rookie of the year.

The 49ers moved into Candlestick Park in 1971. They celebrated with another division title, then marched into

Hall of Fame linebacker Dave Wilcox anchored the 49ers defense for 11 seasons, beginning in 1964.

the playoffs and beat Washington in the first round. That set up a rematch with the Cowboys, this time in Dallas. The outcome wasn't much different, however. Brodie threw three interceptions and the Cowboys' offense did just enough to pull out a 14–3 victory.

The 49ers got another shot at the Cowboys in the 1972 playoffs. The team had started slow, and Brodie suffered an injury. Steve Spurrier stepped in as quarterback and played spectacular football. The Niners won six of their final eight games to clinch their third straight division title. They opened the playoffs against the Cowboys at Candlestick Park. The 49ers were ahead 28–13 in the fourth quarter. But the Cowboys rallied to dash the Niners' hopes again with a 30–28 defeat.

The 49ers would not play in another postseason game for nine years. However, the foundation for the glory years of the 1980s was also being laid.

CANDLESTICK PARK

The San Francisco Giants began playing baseball in Candlestick Park in 1960. It was originally named Bay View Stadium but was changed to Candlestick after a name-the-park contest. The stadium was known for its swirling winds, despite the fact that it had been designed to prevent the wind from having an impact on the game. The 49ers played there until 2013. The stadium was knocked down in 2015.

CHAPTER 3

THE GLORY YEARS

Ohio businessman Ed DeBartolo Jr. bought the 49ers before the start of the 1977 season. His early years as the team owner were miserable. The 49ers failed to win more than five games in any of his first three seasons. The team hit a low in 1978 when it finished 2–14.

The 49ers finished 2–14 in 1979 as well, but there was a different feel to everything taking place. The team had hired Bill Walsh as its new head coach, and he began installing his signature West Coast Offense. The 49ers had also drafted a quarterback from Notre Dame in 1979. His name was Joe Montana.

Montana earned the starting job by the end of the 1980 season. In 1981, he led the 49ers to a 13–3 record and an

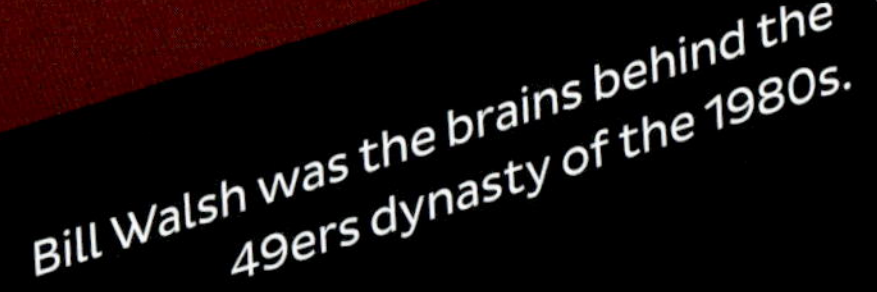
Bill Walsh was the brains behind the 49ers dynasty of the 1980s.

49ERS

"THE GENIUS"

Bill Walsh had to wait until he was 47 before an NFL team hired him as its head coach. Even then, he spent only 10 seasons in that position, all with the 49ers. He made the most of his time. Walsh inherited a poorly managed, losing team. Within just three years, the 49ers were Super Bowl champions and on their way to building a dynasty. During that time, he earned the nickname "The Genius" for his innovative offensive schemes.

Walsh led the 49ers to three Super Bowl victories and six division titles. He was named the NFC's best coach in 1981 and 1984 and won 102 games during his career. Walsh retired from NFL coaching in 1988, before the 49ers' fourth Super Bowl, because he was burned out from coaching. He entered the Hall of Fame in 1993. After a three-year battle with leukemia, Walsh died in 2007. He was 75.

NFC West Division title. The 49ers held off the New York Giants 38–24 in the first round of the playoffs. Then they hosted the Dallas Cowboys—who else?—in the NFC Championship Game. That game would become one of the most memorable games in NFL history.

San Francisco trailed the Cowboys 27–21 with 51 seconds remaining. Montana took the snap inside the Cowboys' 10-yard line. He ran to his right to avoid the rush. Then he launched a pass to the back corner of the end zone. It looked like he was throwing it away to prevent a sack. But wide receiver Dwight Clark seemingly came out of nowhere to make a leaping catch

Dwight Clark punctuates "The Catch" with a spike as the Niners buried years of frustration and futility with their comeback win over Dallas.

in front of Dallas' Everson Walls. The play became known as "The Catch." With a 28–27 victory, the 49ers finally reached the Super Bowl.

At Super Bowl XVI the 49ers defeated the Cincinnati Bengals 26–21. Montana was named the MVP. But the defense made a key stop to preserve the win. Late in the third quarter, the Bengals had four shots at the end zone from inside the 49ers

3-yard line. Each time, the San Francisco defense held them out of the end zone.

Super Bowl XVI was the start of a special era for the 49ers. They were adored by their fans and feared by opponents throughout the 1980s. The 49ers reached the NFC Championship Game again in 1983 but lost to Washington. They came into the 1984 season determined to make up for that loss.

San Francisco dominated its opponents on the way to a 15–1 regular season in 1984. Its only loss was by three points against the Pittsburgh Steelers. In the playoffs, the 49ers knocked off the New York Giants 21–10. Then the defense, led by Ronnie Lott and Fred Dean, sacked Chicago Bears quarterbacks nine times in a 23–0 shutout in the NFC Championship Game.

Up next was a date with the American Football Conference (AFC) champion Miami Dolphins in Super Bowl XIX. Montana noticed that all the pregame talk seemed to center on Miami quarterback Dan Marino, who had shattered NFL single-season records for passing yards and touchdown passes that year. The 49ers quarterback used it as motivation. Montana threw for 331 yards and three touchdowns as San Francisco won 38–16.

The 49ers defeated the Bengals again to win Super Bowl XXIII after the 1988 season. Their decade of dominance ended with another Super Bowl in January 1990. The 49ers went 14–2 during that regular season. After cruising past the Minnesota Vikings and Los Angeles Rams in the playoffs, the 49ers faced quarterback John Elway and the Denver Broncos in Super Bowl XXIV. San Francisco manhandled the Broncos in all aspects of the game in a 55–10 blowout victory.

DEFENSIVE ACE

Ronnie Lott enjoyed a stellar college career as a defensive back at Southern California. Then he was drafted by the 49ers in 1981. Lott had the speed, strength, and intelligence to be a great football player at the NFL level. He was at the heart of the excellent 49ers defenses of the 1980s, and he made more than 1,000 tackles in his career. Lott was a team leader during 10 seasons with the 49ers. He later played for the Los Angeles Raiders and New York Jets. Lott earned a spot in the Pro Football Hall of Fame in 2000. He was a 10-time Pro Bowl selection.

The win secured the 49ers' legacy as the team of the 1980s and one of the greatest NFL dynasties of all time. They won eight division titles in a 10-year period from 1981 to 1990. They made the playoffs nine times during that span and won all four Super Bowls in which they appeared.

CHAPTER 4

PASSING THE TORCH

The 49ers entered the 1990 season as the two-time defending Super Bowl champions. Having already won a Super Bowl under new coach George Seifert, and with the roster still intact, the players were confident they could win a third straight.

It looked promising during the regular season. Joe Montana led the 49ers to a 14–2 record, but the journey was cut short in the playoffs. The 49ers faced the New York Giants in the NFC Championship Game. With San Francisco leading by four in the fourth quarter, Giants defensive lineman Leonard Marshall hit Montana hard. The quarterback suffered a serious injury. He also fumbled the ball. After the Giants recovered it, they kicked a field goal to cut the 49ers'

Quarterback Steve Young did his best to pick up where Joe Montana left off in San Francisco.

lead to 13–12. The Giants added one more field goal to win the game and head to the Super Bowl.

Montana was out for the entire 1991 season. That opened the door for Steve Young. The new quarterback quickly became a star, posting the NFL's best passer rating that season. But Young missed five games with a knee injury, and the 49ers missed the playoffs for the first time in eight seasons.

Young was the MVP of the league in 1992. He led the 49ers to a 14–2 record in the regular season. But they lost to the eventual Super Bowl champion Cowboys 30–20 in the next game. Montana left after that season, but Young's play in 1993 made 49ers fans start to think about the future instead of the past. Young passed for more than 4,000 yards that season and led the team to a 10–6 record. But after beating the Giants in the playoffs, the 49ers lost a close game to Dallas in the NFC Championship Game.

The 49ers added two more superstars for the next season. Defensive back Deion Sanders arrived via free agency from the Atlanta Falcons. And linebacker Ken Norton Jr. left the Cowboys to join the Niners. Sanders intercepted six passes, returning three of them for touchdowns, while Norton led the team in tackles. With the new players, San Francisco had pushed itself

Deion Sanders made his only season in San Francisco a memorable one. He is considered one of the top cornerbacks in NFL history.

to the next level. After a sluggish 3–2 start, the 49ers won 10 straight games and the NFC West title.

The 49ers then beat the Chicago Bears to set up another battle with the Cowboys with a Super Bowl berth on the line.

Out for revenge, the 49ers scored 21 points in the game's first five minutes. They dazzled the Candlestick Park crowd with a 38–28 win over their nemeses.

Young had finally guided the 49ers to a Super Bowl. Now they were heavy favorites against the San Diego Chargers. The 49ers lived up to the billing. Young threw a 44-yard touchdown pass to Jerry Rice early in Super Bowl XXIX, and the 49ers never let go of the momentum. Young finished with a record six touchdown passes in the 49–26 win. The 49ers became the first team to win five Super Bowls.

The 49ers continued to be a contender after the 1994 season. With Young as quarterback, they made the playoffs in each of the next four seasons. But they lost at home to the Green Bay Packers in the NFC Championship Game in January 1998. It soon went downhill from there.

Young retired after missing most of the 1999 season with a severe concussion. The team lost 11 of its 13 remaining games after Young's injury. The 49ers' string of 16 straight 10-win seasons came to a halt as they finished 4–12. It was their first losing record since 1982.

San Francisco recovered a bit, making playoff appearances in 2001 and 2002. But the 49ers struggled to regain the success of the 1980s and early 1990s. Their 2–14 record in 2004 was the worst in the NFL. Dick Nolan's son, Mike Nolan, was named the 49ers coach in 2005. With the number one overall draft pick that year, the 49ers took quarterback Alex Smith from Utah. But the losing seasons continued to pile up.

There were bright spots along the way. Linebacker Patrick Willis immediately established himself as one of the top defensive players in the league after being taken in the first round of the 2007 draft. The 49ers saw a glimmer of hope for the future in 2009. Under coach Mike Singletary, the team finished 8–8, the team's first non-losing record since 2002. Singletary didn't last much longer, however. He went 5–10 in 2010 before being fired. But a new era of success was just around the corner.

T. O.

The 49ers selected talented but controversial wide receiver Terrell Owens in the 1996 NFL Draft. Owens played eight seasons with the 49ers. He racked up more than 8,000 receiving yards and 81 touchdowns during that span. But his time in San Francisco did not end well. He often had trouble getting along with teammates. In 2003, Owens and the 49ers split on bad terms. Owens went on to fill a similar role for the Philadelphia Eagles, Dallas Cowboys, Buffalo Bills, and Cincinnati Bengals. Controversy seemed to follow him wherever he went.

CHAPTER 5

A BUMPY RIDE

The 49ers entered 2011 looking for their first winning season in nine years. Head coach Jim Harbaugh hoped he could end that streak. Harbaugh was a familiar name to those in the area as he had worked as the head coach at nearby Stanford University. The Niners lured him away from the college game and back to the NFL, where he had spent 14 years as a quarterback for four teams.

Harbaugh immediately started working with his starting quarterback. As a former No. 1 overall pick, Alex Smith hadn't lived up to expectations during his first few seasons in the NFL. Harbaugh changed that quickly.

With Smith at quarterback, the 49ers won nine of their first 10 games in 2011. That guaranteed the team's first winning season since 2002. Smith led the offense while

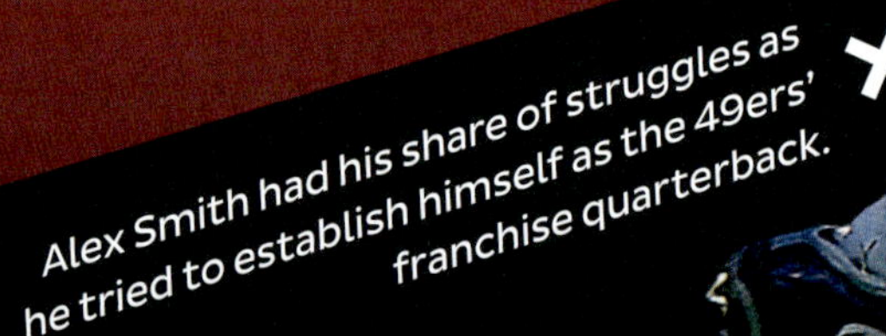

Alex Smith had his share of struggles as he tried to establish himself as the 49ers' franchise quarterback.

A "BEAST"

In the 2007 NFL Draft, the 49ers added a bright young star on defense, too. The 49ers drafted middle linebacker Patrick Willis eleventh overall. The man one scout called a "beast" was named Defensive Rookie of the Year. He had an NFL-best 174 tackles during that rookie season.

Willis quickly established himself as a force on defense. In his first three seasons, he had 467 tackles, nine sacks, and four interceptions. He made the Pro Bowl in each of his first seven seasons. However, Willis retired due to injuries at age 30 in 2015.

Harbaugh and his coaching staff built up a strong defense. Linebackers Patrick Willis and NaVorro Bowman and defensive tackle Justin Smith all put in Pro Bowl efforts as the Niners clinched the NFC West title in Week 13 and finished with a 13–3 record.

The 49ers were tested in their first playoff game against the New Orleans Saints on a sunny, warm January day at Candlestick Park. It came down to the final seconds. San Francisco trailed 32–29 but had reached the New Orleans 14-yard line. Alex Smith hit tight end Vernon Davis for a touchdown. It was a dramatic moment and nearly 30 years to the day after Dwight Clark made "The Catch" in the 1981 NFC Championship Game.

A week later, the 49ers hosted the New York Giants with a trip to the Super Bowl on the line. San Francisco couldn't make that jump, however. The 49ers fumbled two punts, including

Vernon Davis and Jim Harbaugh celebrate after Davis scored the game-winning touchdown against New Orleans in the 2011 NFC Playoffs.

one at their own 24-yard line in overtime that set up the game-winning field goal to send the Giants to the Super Bowl.

COLIN KAEPERNICK

Colin Kaepernick didn't take long to establish himself as a solid quarterback in the NFL. He helped the 49ers reach the Super Bowl after earning the starting quarterback job midway through the 2012 season. Then he led them back to the NFC Championship Game the next season. His level of play fell off slightly following those two successful seasons. But in 2016, Kaepernick made headlines for a different reason. He took a knee during the National Anthem to protest police brutality throughout the country. It was one of the most controversial stories in the news for months. No NFL team signed him when his 49ers contract ended after the 2016 season. However, Kaepernick had plenty of support and raised more than $1 million that he donated to charities.

In 2012 the 49ers started out 6–2. But then Smith suffered a concussion. Second-year backup quarterback Colin Kaepernick got a chance to showcase his skills. Kaepernick rallied the 49ers from 10 points down in the fourth quarter to earn a 24–24 tie with the St. Louis Rams.

The next week Kaepernick threw for 243 yards and two touchdowns in a rout of the Bears in his first NFL start. Because of his strong play, Harbaugh stuck with Kaepernick, who led the 49ers back to the NFC Championship Game. San Francisco flew to Atlanta to face the Falcons. The 49ers fell behind 17–0. But they rallied with two second-half touchdown runs by Frank Gore to win 28–24. San Francisco was back in the Super Bowl.

Colin Kaepernick shows off his running skills against the Atlanta Falcons in the NFC Championship Game.

Super Bowl XLVII was a family affair. San Francisco's opponents, the Baltimore Ravens, were coached by Harbaugh's brother, John. It was the first time two brothers had ever faced each other as head coaches in the Super Bowl. Once again, the 49ers fell behind big. They trailed 28–6 in the second half before rallying. The 49ers cut the deficit to two points early in the fourth quarter but came up just short, losing 34–31 when their last drive fizzled inside the Ravens 10-yard line.

San Francisco and Harbaugh had one more playoff run in them in 2013. It was also the 49ers' last season in Candlestick Park. With Kaepernick at quarterback, San Francisco was once again a tough out in the playoffs. The 49ers went on the road to beat the Green Bay Packers and Carolina Panthers. The NFC Championship Game would be on the road at division rival Seattle. The Seahawks had won the division and had one of the loudest stadiums in the league. But San Francisco didn't go down without a fight. The 49ers kept it close. In the end, a late interception gave Seattle the victory.

The 49ers moved into Levi's Stadium in nearby Santa Clara in 2014. But after an 8–8 season, the team let Harbaugh go. His replacements were underwhelming. Jim Tomsula and Chip Kelly each lasted just one season.

After the 2016 season, San Francisco decided to clean house and bring in a new general manager. The 49ers decided on former NFL defensive back John Lynch, who brought in former Falcons offensive coordinator Kyle Shanahan as head coach.

Midway through the 2017 season, the 49ers acquired quarterback Jimmy Garoppolo in a trade with New England. The 26-year-old had spent his entire career up to that point backing up the great Tom Brady. Garoppolo gave the fans hope

Jimmy Garoppolo arrived in 2017 to take over the Niners' starting quarterback job.

as he led the Niners to victory in their final five games that season. He missed most of the 2018 season with a torn knee ligament, but the 49ers were confident that they'd finally found a franchise quarterback to carry the team into the future.

TIMELINE

1944

A meeting is held on June 4 to discuss the formation of the AAFC. The 49ers become charter members of the league.

1946

In their AAFC debut, the 49ers lose to the New York Yankees 21–7 at Kezar Stadium on September 8.

1949

The 49ers visit the Cleveland Browns in the AAFC championship game on December 11. The 49ers lose 21–7.

1950

The 49ers make their NFL debut on September 17 in a 21–17 loss to the New York Yanks at Kezar Stadium.

1950

After dropping its first five games, San Francisco wins its first NFL game on October 22, defeating the Detroit Lions 28–27.

1957

Team owner Anthony J. "Tony" Morabito dies of a heart attack while watching the 49ers take on the Chicago Bears October 27 at Kezar Stadium.

1960

Coach Red Hickey unveils the shotgun formation against the Baltimore Colts on November 27.

1972

San Francisco plays its final game at Kezar Stadium on January 3, falling 17–10 to the Dallas Cowboys in the NFC Championship Game.

1982

Dwight Clark makes "The Catch" in the end zone as the 49ers stun Dallas 28–27 and advance to their first Super Bowl on January 10.

1982

San Francisco defeats the Cincinnati Bengals 26–21 in Super Bowl XVI on January 24.

Against the Miami Dolphins, the 49ers overcome an early deficit to win 38–16 in Super Bowl XIX on January 20.

1985

Facing the Bengals for the second time in a Super Bowl, the 49ers rally with a 92-yard scoring drive to win 20–16 in Super Bowl XXIII on January 22.

1989

San Francisco defeats the Denver Broncos 55–10 in Super Bowl XXIV on January 28.

1990

The 49ers win a record fifth Super Bowl with a 49–26 win over the San Diego Chargers in Super Bowl XXIX on January 29.

1995

Jim Harbaugh is hired as the head coach of the 49ers.

2011

The 49ers advance to Super Bowl XLVII but fall just short of their sixth title, losing to the Baltimore Ravens 34–31.

2013

Levi's Stadium opens with the Niners losing to the Chicago Bears 28–20 on September 14.

2014

After winning just two games, head coach Chip Kelly is fired and is replaced by Kyle Shanahan.

2016

Quarterback Jimmy Garoppolo arrives via a trade with New England and leads the Niners to five straight wins to end the season.

2017

Tight end George Kittle makes the Pro Bowl after catching 88 passes for 1,377 yards, but the 49ers finish 4–12.

2018

QUICK STATS

FRANCHISE HISTORY

1946–1949 (AAFC)
1950– (NFL)

SUPER BOWLS *(wins in bold)*

1981 (XVI), **1984 (XIX)**, **1988 (XXIII)**, **1989 (XXIV)**, **1994 (XXIX)**, 2012 (XLVII)

AAFC CHAMPIONSHIP GAMES *(1946–49)*

1949

NFC CHAMPIONSHIP GAMES *(since 1970 AFL-NFL merger)*

1970, 1971, 1981, 1983, 1984, 1988, 1989, 1990, 1992, 1993, 1994, 1997, 2011, 2012, 2013

KEY COACHES

Jim Harbaugh (2011–14): 44–19–1, 5–3 (playoffs)
George Seifert (1989–96): 98–30, 10–5 (playoffs)
Bill Walsh (1979–88): 92–59–1, 10–4 (playoffs)

KEY PLAYERS *(position, seasons with team)*

Dwight Clark (WR, 1979–87)
Roger Craig (RB, 1983–90)
Vernon Davis (TE, 2006–15)
Fred Dean (DE, 1981–85)
Frank Gore (RB, 2005–14)
Colin Kaepernick (QB, 2011–16)
Ronnie Lott (DB, 1981–90)
Joe Montana (QB, 1979–92)
Joe Perry (RB, 1948–60, 1963)
Jerry Rice (WR, 1985–2000)
Alex Smith (QB, 2005–12)
Y. A. Tittle (QB, 1951–60)
Dave Wilcox (LB, 1964–74)
Patrick Willis (LB, 2007–14)
Steve Young (QB, 1987–99)

HOME FIELDS

Levi's Stadium (2014–)
Candlestick Park (1971–2013)
Kezar Stadium (1946–70)

*All statistics through 2018 season

QUOTES AND ANECDOTES

When the 49ers hired coach Jim Tomsula prior to the 2015 season, they brought aboard a man who had worked his way from the bottom up. Tomsula has done some odd jobs in his career including working as a janitor and a doormat salesman. He started off well by winning his first game as 49ers coach. But the Niners went 5–11 that year and Tomsula was fired after just one season as head coach.

"Well, I'm an old country boy, and I used to go hunting with a shotgun. How about we call it the shotgun?"

—Former 49ers head coach Red Hickey on the new offensive alignment he unveiled in 1960

"This is just a tremendous loss for all of us, especially to the Bay Area because of what he meant to the 49ers. For me personally, outside of my dad he was probably the most influential person in my life. I am going to miss him."

—Joe Montana on the death of Bill Walsh

In a *Monday Night Football* game in Seattle in October 2002, 49ers wide receiver Terrell Owens pulled a permanent marker out of his sock after catching a touchdown pass. He then proceeded to autograph the ball and hand it to his financial adviser. The adviser was sitting in an end zone luxury suite rented by Shawn Springs, the cornerback Owens had just beaten on the play.

GLOSSARY

hall of fame
A place built to honor noteworthy achievements by athletes in their respective sports.

legacy
Something of importance that came from someone in the past.

merge
Join with another to create something new, such as a company, a team, or a league.

momentum
The strength or force that allows something to continue or to grow stronger.

red zone
The area on a football field between the end zone and the 20-yard line.

shotgun
A formation in which the quarterback lines up 3 to 5 yards behind the center and takes the snap in the air.

T-formation
A type of offense that uses three running backs plus a quarterback.

West Coast Offense
An offense that uses a variety of formations to confuse a defense. It uses a short passing game designed to control the football.

MORE INFORMATION

BOOKS

Cohn, Nate. *San Francisco 49ers*. New York: AV2 by Weigl, 2018.

Graves, Will. *The Best NFL Offenses of All Time*. Minneapolis, MN: Abdo Publishing, 2014.

Zappa, Marcia. *San Francisco 49ers*. Minneapolis, MN: Abdo Publishing, 2015.

ONLINE RESOURCES

To learn more about the San Francisco 49ers, visit **abdobooklinks.com** or scan this QR code. These links are routinely monitored and updated to provide the most current information available.

PLACES TO VISIT

Levi's Stadium
4900 Marie P. DeBartolo Way
Santa Clara, CA 95054
415-464-9377
levisstadium.com

The 49ers' home since 2014 also hosted Super Bowl 50.

Pro Football Hall of Fame
2121 George Halas Dr. NW
Canton, OH 44708
330-456-8207
profootballhof.com

This hall of fame and museum highlights the greatest players and moments in the history of the NFL.

INDEX

ABOUT THE AUTHOR

Tony Hunter is a writer from Castle Rock, Colorado. This is his first children's book series. He lives with his daughter and his trusty Rottweiler, Dan.